T0196265

Inside a Crazy Mind

MALCOLM WASHINGTON
IS THE RULER OF RHYME

authorHOUSE®

AuthorHouse™
1663 Liberty Drive
Bloomington, IN 47403
www.authorhouse.com
Phone: 1-800-839-8640

First published by AuthorHouse   09/02/2011

ISBN: 978-1-4670-3345-9 (sc)

Printed in the United States of America

INDEX OF POEMS

To my family, my sisters, Cynthia and Annette, my parents, grandparents, godparents and Bubbie, who embraced the weirdness of my mind.

Acknowledgement

Thank you to all my extended family and friends who believed in the craziness. To my eighth grade Language Arts teacher, Mrs. Violate who introduced me to poetry. To my buddy, Mr. Simmons, one of the best teachers you could ever ask for, thank you for your support and help during my recuperation. To my middle school vice principal, Mrs. Mathis, thank you for your help during my ailment. To my brother, Matthew Schweiger, and his family, true friends until the end, thanks for being there. To my friend, Chris Wilson, a fellow writer who has a comedic style that inspires me daily . . . even when he is not being funny. To Bubbie, who probably does not want to be mentioned, but is a positive influence on me and the way I treat others. I thank my sisters, Cynthia and Annette, who read my poetry and stories before they were even popular and encouraged me to write more. I would also like to thank my godparents, Austine and John, who knew my poetry was something great. Special thanks to my mom and dad, for all the hard work and support, I could not have done it without you. And most of all, thank you God for healing me and helping me become who I am today.

Your Choice

Have you ever done something so crazy?
Insane?
Just a little bit, maybe,
Ever try something so impossible?

Have you ever done something so out there?
It would make everyone stop and stare,
Then here's what you do . . .

Be spontaneous, creative, out there,
Be artistic, imaginative, and don't care,
What people say or do,
And remember who you are, is up to you!

Destiny

Did ever wonder from time to time,
What would happen if you changed the history of your life?
Stop every tear you've ever cried,
Make a plan to change time?

Did you ever think you would make it far?
Did you ever dream you would be a star,
Driving one of those fancy cars?

Did you ever think, if it was up to me,
I would be whoever I wanted to be, therefore, changing your destiny,
Even make it something crazy, possibly?
You may be thinking "you're not the boss of me,"
And you're right because it's your destiny.

One of a Kind Girl

She's amazing,
Got to thank the Lord,
Yes praise Him,
For this wonderful . . .
One of a kind girl.

She's so crazy,
Spontaneous, fun, I must say,
My heart pounds ever so loudly,
Every time I see her,
She's a one of a kind girl.

Sparks start flying,
Her energy's electrifying,
I'm telling you that I'm not lying,
Take a look and tell me if
She's a one of a kind girl.

She's so much fun,
I met her in the summer sun,
Chances were a million to one,
Of finding a girl like her,
A one of a kind girl.

Your Life

You can't see it,
You can't feel it,
But you know it's there.
Rushing past you,
Rushing through you,
Rushing through your hair.

Some can't stand it,
Others can't take it,
Your potential,
Your talent,
They can't erase it.

Do what you love,
Love what you do,
It's your life it's all up to you.
So if you're feeling down,
Or maybe a bit blue,
Fix it, change it,
It's all up to you.

The Mystery of Mr. Bell

Here's a scary story I would like to tell,
About a certain Mr. Bell.
Heard a noise up in his attic one day,
Came down with hair the shade of gray!
Mumbling of horrible things he had seen,
Then his face turned a sickly green.
He laid on the sofa to rest his head,
Next thing you know, the poor fellow was dead.

Take A Good Look

Take a good look,
LOOK BACK!
What do see, in fact,
What do you know, for sure?
This is what happens with war!

Look at what you see,
Nothing! but rubble and debris!
This world was once great,
Then it filled with hate!

It is tragic indeed,
All for selfishness and greed,
This happened slowly, you know,
Now, won't you . . .

Take a good look!
Look back,
See all the blood and gore,
This is what happens . . .
This is what happens with war.

"The Legend of Daniel Bone"

Tell you about a musician,
That isn't too well known,
At the age of 9,
All he wanted was a saxophone.

He bought one and began to play,
Not one lesson but he played beautifully,
He looked at all the dropped jaws,
Which quickly changed into a great applause.

At age eleven,
He was as good as anybody,
Could play any instrument from A-Z.

Then one day he just disappeared,
No word of him far or near.

Some claim he died all alone,
Some say he's at his house,
Practicing his saxophone.

He never writes his name on his music,
So the next time you see music by "Artist Unknown"
Sure enough it's by Daniel Bone.

You and I

You and me,
We're meant to be,
You can tell,
And I can see.

When I look into your sparkling eyes,
It's fair to say,
They hypnotize.

You and me we're meant to be,
You can feel it in the air,
I can tell by your energy.

You're my better half, you see,
I can tell because
You lighten my mood incredibly.

Now, I just need you to see . . .
You and I are meant to be,
I'll show you,
If you're willing to see.

Halloween Dreams

The wind blows the leaves,
And brushes your hair,
Full moon rises,
Sun sets with care.
But on this night, do beware,
There is also danger in the air.

Once you go to sleep,
Darkness sees a chance to creep,
Into your mind . . . where dreams live,
Horrible nightmares it shall give.

Tonight!
Dreams and nightmares begin to fight,
Howls and laughs,
Shrieks and smiles,
Beautiful rainbows and creepy phone misdials.

Come close together for one night,
Just try to hang on until the morning light,
So proclaims The Ruler of Fright!

Blended Colors

All the colors start to blend,
Everything starts over again.
Life never ends,
It just changes the way it begins.

You wake up everyday,
So you can escape a world full of gray,
To a place where you are safe,
Yet you still dream of a better place
Where blended colors you embrace.

Breaking Free

Who are you today?
Are you even yourself right now?
Are you letting all your stress and problems bring you down?
Take a minute,
And just breathe.

If you're the person I described right now,
Then do this thing for me,
Go out and paint the town.
Red, blue, or green,
That doesn't matter I'll tell you that now.

And now that you're free,
Of all chains and binds,
You have the choice,
To leave your old life behind.

I can only give advice,
But I cannot control what you do,
So what I'm trying to say is,
The choice up to you.

The Ruler of Rhyme

My mind works differently,
Than others do,
It's a new day,
And it's fair to say,
I got a new attitude.

I feel like I can fly,
I'm ready to be me,
And shoot for the sky,
Gonna show the world who I can be.

And I don't know why;
But I feel creativity
Rush through my brain,
I know it sounds a little insane,

But just relax,
You'll be just fine,
This a new era . . .
The one of
The Ruler of Rhyme!

The Best Dance

I step through the door,
The music was pumping,
Everyone there started jumping.
I met some friends and started to hang out,
Then everyone began to shout.

We guys looked good,
The girls looked great,
The DJ rocked the entire state.
He was awesome,
He could break dance,
He challenged us but we didn't stand a chance.

Once he turned it down slow everyone was shocked,
Then, I saw a chance to make this my dance,
And I had to make it rock.

There was a girl pretty as can be,
While some wore make up it seemed she had a natural beauty,
So I went up and asked her, "Would you like to dance with me?"

She wore a white dress,
And with that she said "yes,"
Now, I admit that was the best.

Well, the party went on,
They played great songs.
There was no regret,
That was it,
The best time yet!

Star Power

Look up,
Look at the sky,
Look at the stars,
My oh my.
You can tell everything's just fine,
Perfect weather for a Friday night,
Hanging out be alright,
Stick around make a wish tonight,
And then watch your dreams take flight,
On this perfect starry night.

Crazy Man

Do you see it?
What has happened to him?
Nice on the outside, but on the inside, BOOM!

He rushes in a ZOOM!
He's bursting out of his room!

He once was glad, but then BOOM!
He lost everything I assume,
Nice on the outside, but inside KAZOOM!

His head is hurting,
He's screaming at a shoe,
And he has nothing and all because of you,
You, You, YOU!
BOOM!

Cry on a Rainy Day

Rain is pouring down on us, there is nothing we can do,
Sorry to say it, but that is true,
And when the skies start to turn gray,
All we can do is cry on a rainy day.

Your words are like lightning,
Flashing before my eyes,
Don't you know that it's frightening,
To hear those thunderous cries?

The pain is like hail, falling from the sky,
Hitting harder each and every time,
It wasn't a good way to end this,
It was a terrible goodbye.

And now, there is nothing I can do or say,
All I can do now . . .
Is cry on a rainy day.

On a Dream Cloud

On a dream cloud,
Way above the skies,
There's a world not known by many people eyes.

A world of your own,
You just have to close your eyes,
It doesn't matter
If it's day or if it's night.

A dream cloud,
Never says its goodbyes,
It's your world,
Yes, your personal paradise.

I know that life's hard,
It is very hard sometimes,
But all you have to do realize . . .
You can be on your dream cloud if you close your eyes.

On a dream cloud,
Way above the skies,
There's a world so beautiful,
That it would make you cry.

Silence

Tick tock,
Hear that clock?
As it sets out a sigh.
So silent, it would make a grown man cry.
So quiet and peaceful like a star lit sky.
Not a whisper,
Nor a sound,
No, not so far,
We just sit there in silence,
Confused and in awe.

Tears

One by one,
They fall from above,
One by one,
They start to run.

Tear after tear,
Year after year,
They just come,
But never in ones.

Like a big and stormy cloud,
Crushing down, onto a beautiful flower mound,

Visiting cities and small towns,
From both the sad and happy now.

Not Your Average Girl

We're one in the same that is for sure,
Being together is the ultimate cure.
Hanging around up at my school,
Just talking about what we should do.
Things go right when I'm with her,
This is not your average girl.
She likes things I like to do,
She's real smart and pretty too.
We both laugh at the same things,
One in the same forever it seems.

Not to be Controlled

They have to have two things to win,
The eye of tiger and the heart of a champion,
But I must say they can't be gone,
If they are, things are wrong.

So if you're thinking you know,
Then I'm ready, so let's go.
I've been doing 5k's since I was ten years old,
And honestly I'm not to be controlled.

I have a drive; that is what leads me to win,
Come down and I'll take you for a spin,
And if you don't believe me truth be told,
I'm telling you now that I'm not to be controlled

So if you're thinking you can take me down,
Watch yourself or you'll be on the ground,
I work with weights and I run too,
If you mess with me; I'll mess with you,
And even when I'm old and alone,
I'll still be ready,
And never controlled!

Heart Broken Until the Last Heartbeat

Heart broken,
Yeah, he went a little insane,
He tries to stop crying,
But it comes down like a rain.

He feels so lost,
He wished he had been closer,
He looks up at her picture,
By the movie poster.

He runs out,
Goes to the cliff where
Some of his friends made him jump once
On a stupid dare.
As a matter of fact, I think his first date was there.
With a girl by the name of . . . never mind,
You don't care,
One foot on the ground,
One in the air.

She was the reason for his heart to beat,
That's what he said,
Isn't that sweet?

She's gone now,
That's all that matters,
Is it really worth having his brain splattered?

His heart raced as he jumped,
Bump, Bump,
Bump, Bump,
Bump, Bump,
THUMP!

"All the Time in the World"

We have all the time in the world
To do what we want to do,
We have all the time in the world
To make our dreams come true,
We have all the time in the world
To try something new,
But I only have this one moment with you.

Hear the Stories of the Mad

Hear the stories of the mad,
They can tell you why they're sad.
Feel the darkness and the pain,
The insanity started with one man who missed his train,

One man, Johnny,
Saved the day,
But he still had debts to pay,
'Til he fell in the snow,
Ice can burn, don't you know?
His pain shattered his brain,
And now he's insane,
The stories are darker than they seem,
Because at night you'll hear him scream,
This is what happens don't you know,
When you've been buried in the snow,

Hear the stories of the mad,
Understand why they're sad,
Feel the darkness and the pain,
In the mind of the insane,

Hear the story of Joey King,
The man who had everything,
Took his boat out to ride the tides,
He was alert at all times,
Until he heard some Sirens sing,
His boat crashed hear his scream,
See him in the light house's beam,

Hear the stories of mad,
Hear their cries?
Aren't they sad?

It may seem a little gory
But here's another story,
Of a man who ran away,
With a crow,
It's a sad story,

Ran out food,
And starved dry,
With no shelter,
Surely he'd die,

Then his bird flew away,
And came back another day,
And in it's search of food,
It ate its host,
How crude,
And it laughed while it chewed,

You can hear another scream,
Because this is all one man's dream,
He went crazy that day,
And now you can hear him say,
"There's a story don't you know?
About a man . . . who died in the snow?"

Hopes this helps you feel their pain,
And get into the mind of the insane.

Peace of Mind

All of life shatters,
Before your eyes,
Hear all the madness,
See it burn like fires.

To all life's secrets,
You hold the key,
To change all of your reality.

Go into the darkness,
Only to see the light,
Then your world shatters,
Your imagination comes to life.

You'll be okay,
You'll be just fine,
Because the key you hold is the key to
Peace of Mind.

Hero

I'll tell you just what this world needs,
With all its selfishness and greed.

We just a need a certain somebody to be a . . . hero,
If they please.

Now someone step up if they will,
Why is everyone motionless and still?
Are you scared of the world, is that the deal?
You created this monster,
And it can kill.

Look at the tax budgets,
Building up a monstrous hill,
People dying because they are ill,
Children so hungry they'd eat anything and will.

So look at what the world has come to be,
That's why we need a hero,
So is there anybody?

Wishing Star

Stars that shine, deep in the night,
Listen, please, if you might.
Let it be, if you may,
A star shines for somebody, today.

So in their life a light has shone,
Leading to a brighter road,
Let it be by tomorrow,
You help get rid of their sorrow.

Stars light,
Stars of night,
Let your everlasting light,
Guide us to a new day,
Let the light you shine lead the way!

I Hope You Knew

Tell you about a girl,
One of the greatest in the world,
Life's never bland,
No, not with her,
This is true,
So, I hope you knew . . .

You were the sun,
When I was down and low,
I thought of you,
You were the light at the end of the tunnel,
That helped me through,

And I hope that you knew,
Everything I do,
I'm still thinking of you,
Do you think of me, too?

I should have known,
Better to write this poem,
Because you can probably see right through,
But all the words that I just told you,
I guarantee that each is word is true.

One Moment

Sometimes I wish time would freeze,
That the world would stop,
For one moment,
One moment for me,
Please.

Sometimes it seems like life is nothing but a dream,
So things aren't always what they seem . . .

I've been lost in a dream,
Where creativity controls me,
Rushing through every part of me,
To see if I can break free.

If I Could...

If I could do anything,
I'd be with you right now,
Doesn't matter when,
Doesn't matter where,
Doesn't matter how.

All I need is for your eyes to meet mine,
Then we could leave all our troubles behind.

You smile's brighter than the sun in May,
I think about it more every night and day.

If I could do anything,
I'd give this poem to you,
So that you could see the way I feel is true.

Shades of Gray

I thought darkness controlled everything,
Clouds in the sky would make it dark all day,
You dream you're flying,
But in reality it seems,
You're only falling without wings.

Life can be dull,
What else can I say?
The lightest it can feel sometimes is gray.

But, if you think . . . time after time,
You'll see the sun come out to shine.

And If your world is filled with shades of gray,
Just remember tomorrow is a new day.

One Stormy Night

You don't know what it is,
Could be the cold air,
But all of the sudden it's touching your hair,

You're home all alone,
With a disconnected phone,
And nearby you can hear a moan,
That's quite strange since you're alone.

You try to stay brave though you can't hide,
That you're afraid deep down inside,
You shriek and cry,
Because there's no one else here tonight.

Teeth lash out of the darkness,
And retract just in time,
You step back,
Scared out of your mind.

Your instincts start to kick in,
It starts all over again,
He tries to scratch and bite you,
You struggle to put up a fight,
But, hey, what can you expect,
On this stormy night?

I Won't Give Up

I won't give up,
I'll tell you why,
I'll spread my wings,
And touch the sky.

I won't give up,
I'm telling you,
The words I'm saying are all true

Greatness lurks in us all,
So why not fly instead of fall,
I'm on my way,
I'm not going to stop,
Until they say,
"You've reached the top!"

I won't give up,
No, not yet,
The time hasn't come,
The date isn't set,
I'm on my way,
To show the world . . .

I won't give up,
I'll you why,
I haven't found a reason not to try.

"Stone Cold Road"

I've heard of a stone cold road,
Once belonging to a heart of gold,
And now before I sing this song,
I ask if you are a small child please move along,

This man walks a lonely road,
His heart filled with ice and cold,
Worked in a graveyard they say,
Always happy,
Never gray.

Until one dark night,
His task was to bury his wife,

But let's start from the beginning of that night.
It all started with a fight,
One cried out in the middle of the night,
Other stuck sobbing with a knife,
While the other cried out in pain,
That night he just left on a train,

For now you hear him cry,
Every night to his wife, it's his goodbye,
Kill himself?
He's already tried,
But you can't when you've already died,
Inside,

Now he walks a lonely road,
With no name of his own,
Voice much like a toad's,
He just runs away,
No house to call a home,

He dying down inside,
Runs so he can find a place to die,
Because of what he had done,
He stays in the shadows,
No need for the sun

No, he won't let go of the past they say,
Walks in memory of that day,
Sadly he's not insane,
That only would start to ease the pain,

Now he walks a stone cold road,
Heart of ice and burned by the cold,
At night, you can hear him howl,
If think it's the wind,
Well, you know better now.

Inside Dreams

In my dreams,
Ideas go on and on,
In my dreams,
Angels sing their song.

You can't tell,
But deep in your sleep at night,
That's when you're the most creative and bright.

Your dreams may not be the same,
You could dream of stars or a planet far away.
If you ask me, you know what I'd say,
Life is a dream,
So be happy.

Killed with Kindness.

I guess it's true what they say,
No good deed goes unpunished,
I think of that more and more everyday.

Honestly,
Look at the world today,
Filled with destruction,
Well, what can I say?

Yeah, I killed them with kindness,
I'm sorry to say,
So just slap on the cuffs and take me away.

But there's one more thing I've got to say,
"So . . . how many crimes do you hear like this everyday?

Drowned in love rather than burned with hate,
Hugged to death,
Showing care and compassion,
Am I the only one left?"

There's a better way than all this madness,
When it comes to enemies,
Just simply,
Kill them with kindness.

Soul Mate

Listen, though it may sound strange,
In a second you've changed,
The way I feel,
It's so real,
I couldn't deal
With life without you,
For this is surely true,
Ever since we met,
There has been no regret,
You have filled my heart with glee,
Soon we will be together happily.

Change is Going to Come

The blue skies have all gone,
Now, all we see is gray,
Working to the bone,
In a dull factory.

Used to be skies,
So bright and blue,
But now tearing eyes,
And a dark point of view.

The hardships are getting harder,
The pain of it all,
Feels like hours are getting longer,
Packed inside this small stall.

But I'll tell you, my friend,
One by one,
Things will be changing,
And a change is going to come.

"Christmas"

Hear the sounds of their joy,
Little girls and little boys,
Rushing to the Christmas tree,
To see what Santa brought thee.

Going to church Christmas day,
Hear the sound of them pray,
And tell the story of that glorious day,
Thanking Him in every way.

Smiling bright as though,
The world has many friends and no foe,
Merry Christmas and Peace on Earth to you all,
May you have good fortune befall.

My Father

My father, you are so great,
You have shown me how I can remain in a calm state.
When things are horrible you remain calm,
I must say, dear father,
That you have it all.

It may seem sometimes that I mope,
But, oh dear father, you give me hope.
You give me a drive like no other,
To want to win against another.
You see dear father you have it all,
You're handsome, happy and tall.

I must say, you push me to do my best,
You bring out the good in me and leave the rest.
I know sometimes things seem bad,
But I know you can fix it because you are my dad.

For you, I must applaud dear father for being so clever,
I must say you are the best dad ever!
I hope to follow in your footsteps someday,
I send my love and my praise,
This ode is to you, oh, father of days.

Be You

When clouds start to clear,
You can see how the sun shines,
And when the sun goes down,
Some start to frown,
While . . .

I stay up late at night,
To watch the stars shine bright,
They'll talk to you if the time is right.

And when they will say . . .
"We may be stars but we don't always shine,
Look at yourself and realize,
Your life is ahead of you,
And waiting out that door,
While we are in the sky you can do so much more."

I stay up late at night,
To watch the stars,
Shining brightly like fancy cars.

And don't you know what they would say,
"Look, at us, look how bright we shine,
We look down on you all the time,
But look at you,
Look at where you are!
To tell the truth it isn't that far,
You can join us one of these days,
You will receive glory and great praise,
There is only one thing you must do,
That is, be creative and be you."

A Friend

Let it go,
Just let it go,
Sorrowful days and nights,
Filled with woe.

Dark Days of Morning come and go.
But in the end,
They'll pick you up when you are down,
And save you each day,
Just by sticking around,
And when you're with them,
It is impossible to frown,

So when you're beat,
And feel weak,
And don't have the strength to speak,
Even when you're knocked down and off your feet,
There will always be someone to understand,
They're a friend!

A Warning

"Fire,
Destruction,
Pain,
Corruption,"
That's all he will say,
All night and all day,
No one knows why,
They just hear his great cry.

"Fire,
Destruction,
Pain,
Corruption,"
Making no sense anymore,
Eyes burning,
Head on the floor.
Time and time again,
He'll smile and then . . .
He'll warn you of the end.

"Fire,
Destruction,
Pain,
Corruption,"
It comes down to this,
Is he insane or a wiz?

"Fire,
Destruction,
Pain,
Corruption."

One Life

So I've come all this way,
I've come so far today,
Sore eyes,
And legs feel like clay.

Swim on to another day,
Cleansing all my bad deeds away,
Jumping through a ring of fire,
Some might even say.
To go and clear my good name,
To take the dark out of the gray.

To help a life,
To find one and save . . .
One life each and everyday.

So I've come,
Through the pouring rain,
To go and cleanse and save . . .
One life everyday.

Only to finally be saved,
All souls will be cleansed,
Dark shadows washed away,
So I've come to those who need me,
And I've come to help them today.

Madness

Conflicting issues in my head,
As I lay here in my bed.
As I remember what they said,
And I fill with dread.
Questions surround my head,
But no questions answered, instead,
Only more thoughts . . . leading to madness,
But it's only in my head.

Originality

The world's lacking originality,
I wonder how this could be,
That was sarcasm,
Let me tell you what I see . . .

Seems like now,
Not just in schools,
But in every place,
The colors are being drained,
And numbers replace your face.

Do you want to be known as student #43?
Or office order # 60?
Honestly,
If you can't even say our name,
Doesn't that mean we're all the same?

Just dull, uninteresting people,
You know everyone may need to be treated the same,
But, we're not numbers, no; we're not all the same,
We're just not colors,
We all have names,
NAMES!

The Perfect Night

I looked up into her eyes,
They sparkled like the night skies.
Her hair fell like a cascade,
It did.

We danced all night it seemed,
Under the moon's bright beam.
Silver and full,
It shined perfectly.

Though nights were once a depressing scene,
It's never been that way for me.
The night's stars shine so brilliantly,
That even a blind man could see exactly what I mean.

A perfect night it seemed,
Almost like a dream,
One day I'll tell you exactly what I mean,
Because no night is this perfect,
No not usually,
A perfect night is normally just a dream.

Silver Moon

The silver moon shines tonight,
So beautifully and so bright,
With stars lit around it,
Beautiful as it can get.

But a silver moon at night,
Sets the mood just right,
It's like an angel from above,
Showering the world with light and love.

So every night and day,
I sit and I pray for another night,
Under the silver moon's beautiful light.

"Karma or Vengeance?"

Here is a story of a butcher named Jack,
And one day a man came by,
He said, "If I don't get food soon I will die,"
Jack brought down a bag and said,
"That's not my problem Mr. Fred,"

Fred opened up the bag and what he found,
Was hair a nice color brown,
He opened more and saw a face,
He whispered to himself, "I got to leave this place,"
The butcher laughed and chopped his meat,
"Hey, if you want I've got the matching feet,"

No remorse for the weird creep,
The next year came round;
The butcher was sitting in his room,
Gazing at the full moon,
Not a knock at his door,
But a *scratch* instead,
A man at the door,
One called Fred,
But Fred was dead,
But a smile on his face,

The butcher screamed and hopped back,
He ran up the stairs,
"Now, listen Jack!
If you think I'm revolting look back!
Then look at what you've done to me!
All for some quick money,"
The butcher ran up to the meat locker,
"Oh, please just leave me alone,"
More zombies behind grumbling like a dial tone,
He went down stairs scared but not alone,
And you won't guess what he saw,
The man who had starved was very much alive,
Smiling and standing tall,
Now every 13th of Friday the butcher hides,
Karma or Vengeance,
I'll let you decide.

Moving On

Everyone's . . .
Grown up,
Moved on,
While I'm stuck singing sad songs,
Wondering "how this can be?"

I hang out with my friends,
Once a get home,
The fun ends.
So I go and watch TV,
But I still feel so empty.

Little girls, little boys,
Quiet down,
And stop the noise.
Being an only child isn't as great as I'd thought it to be,
So please, listen to me.

Older brothers and sisters who are out on their own,
I just ask that you remember to pick up your phone,
And call your siblings,
Who feel so alone,
Because I guarantee,
They're up waiting for you to come home.

Legacy

So here I am today,
You aren't going to stop me, now,
I'm going save this place,
I'm going save this town.

Believe in who I am,
Believe in what you see,
Believe in who you are,
Believe in legacy.

My heart and my soul,
Together perfectly,
Are stronger than before,
Stronger than can be,
The power that I know,
Runs like a river through me,
Achieving all my goals,
Setting me free.

I have no doubt,
Who I'm going to be,
Stronger than most,
Better than you've seen,
I'm going to show this town,
The best I can be.

Go ahead knock me down,
Later on you'll see,
What I'm saying now,
What I wish to be,
Will come true,
So says my legacy.

Goodbye

There is so much I wish I could tell you,
But only so much I can say,
I'm sorry but this has become the only way.

Do you know, why letting go,
May be the hardest thing to do?
So I have decided to go,
And leave this choice with you.

I wish things were different than before,
Alas, like a wave I've crashed to a different shore,
Feelings change, that I've always known,
I'm sorry to leave you all alone.

What a Nice Day

Just a beautiful bright shining day,
Everything's fine and going my way,
Nothing is going to stop me,
No, not today.

Sitting around like there's nothing to do,
That's bad for both me and you.
Let's explore the world,
Do something new.

If your world's the same, life can be quite blue.
So go change ideas, change your point of view,
So go out in the world,
Do something new.

Something Out There

Smiles all around here,
I don't know what to do,
Some say just smile when I'm blue.

I don't understand it,
Maybe it isn't true,
Maybe there's something out there,
That I never knew,
And maybe it's something like you.

I see you're different,
You know it too,
It's fine by me,
And by you.

Maybe there's something out there,
Something I never knew,
And maybe that something,
That something is you.

My Future

I'll tell you now,
Who I am and who I'll be,
Intertwined,
And later on, one day you'll finally see . . .

Everything's going to be alright,
And I will be who I always wanted to be.
One moment to prove myself,
If you would please . . .

Not much at all,
Just one chance is all I need . . .
To show how different I can truly be . . .
To show you who I'm going to be.

Music

A song to sing,
A tune to hum,
Some bells to ring,
And drums to drum.

Musicians here,
And more to come,
To show that they truly care,
The sounds of music are in the air,
Listen and you can hear it, everywhere.

Words Can Kill

Words can hurt,
Like sharp claws,
Or even like a creature's jaws.
Words can be monsters,
That makes you a killer,
Doesn't it?
After all you're the one who said it,
Sending them free,
Into the mind of an innocent,

You'll forget about it in a minute or perhaps a little more,
But the person you hurt wishes they were never born,
See, words can kill,
Because they're monsters,
What does that make you?
Other than a murder,

Once they're free,
They can't be controlled,
They'll just eat at the person's happiness and soul,

So the monsters are free,
And the murderer gets away,
Guess what!
This happens almost everyday,
That's the end,
Sorry it's not happy.

Showdown at Sunrise

Back in the days when all men wore a frown,
A mysterious stranger came riding into town.

Fought all the outlaws, banished them away,
With a hat the shade of brown,
And a beard the shade of gray.

Until one dark day,
A new outlaw came into town,
Frightened women and children,
Knocked all the men down.

The outlaw threatened to shoot the Salon owner,
His eyes flaming,
The outlaw warned the man with a dark hiss,
"You better getta praying."

He laughed as he left, only for the sheriff to say,
"This is my town so get gone,"
He turned around and said,
"We'll settle this at dawn!"

Graduation

Graduation,
All across the nation,
Will have our hearts racing,
And all of us pacing.

As we wait there,
Standing in the warm air,
We begin to stare,
We look at the chairs,
Searching for our parents, somewhere.

As we leave here,
Some may shed a tear,
For now we face fear,
Now that high school is near.

But we keep a strong face,
Ready to embrace,
Challenges in the next place,
And dreams that we will chase,
We leave with grace.

My Summer Break

Summer, yes, summer is there any time more fun?
You get to relax,
And play jacks in the smiling summer sun,
But last summer was greater, you see.

I boarded a ship like no other,
This ship was tall and wide enough as well,
We had joy and played and had fun,
In the old summer sun.
I had fun and played and, boy,
It made the last of the summer days swell.

But even perfect days have to end,
Good bye summer,
My old friend.
When finally it went down I surrendered,
School is coming soon I remembered,

So when the sun goes down I see it wink,
And the last of the summer days went by,
And I stare there blankly at the dark sky thinking to myself "why?"

Coming Soon . . .

Simon the Hero

(A Children's Story)

"Yes, but I'm in no condition to fight
Not anyone especially the black knight,"
The king sighed, his voice small as sand,
"If you defeat the knight I'll let you rule the land,"
Simon blinked, confused and bewildered,
"Sire, surely you wouldn't expect a villager . . ."

About the Author

As a child Malcolm had difficulty riding a bicycle, playing sports or tolerating loud sounds, but could write stories. At eleven, Malcolm was diagnosed with hydrocephalous. In 2009, he experienced a shunt malfunction, an infection and three brain surgeries. As a result, Malcolm underwent physical, occupational and speech therapies. Prior to graduating with his eighth grade class, Malcolm was introduced to poetry in his Language Arts class. His first poem "My Summer Break" was published in *The Gold Edition: 2010 Poetry Collection,* a collection of poetry from students across the United States. His creative process for poetry writing includes using rhythmic patterns that he hears in his head. His poems are relatable, humorous, thought provoking and sometimes creepy for an individual his age. A select group of individuals have enjoyed his poetic style and now he wants to expand his audience. His unique poetic style is entertaining to adults as well as children. He plans to pursue a career in psychology. He enjoys helping individuals and believes his knowledge and experience with brain trauma can help interpret the thoughts of an unstable mind.